I'm Happy Being Me

Children's Poems and Prayers

Cecelia Holloway

Trilogy Christian Publishers
A Wholly Owned Subsidary of Trinity Broadcasting Network
2442 Michelle Drive
Tustin, CA 92780

For information, address Trilogy Christian Publishing
Rights Department, 2442 Michelle Drive, Tustin, Ca 92780.
Trilogy Christian Publishing/ TBN and colophon are trademarks of Trinity Broadcasting Network.

For information about special discounts for bulk purchases, please contact Trilogy Christian Publishing.

Manufactured in the United States of America

10 9 8 7 6 5 4 3 2 1

Library of Congress Cataloging-in-Publication Data is available.

ISBN 978-1-64773-733-7 (Print Book)
ISBN 978-1-64773-734-4 (ebook)

Special Thank-You

I want to say a special thank-you to my wonderful husband. Your love, support, and encouragement over the years have given me strength and energy to keep creating and being myself and loving what I do.

To my six children, watching you become the fine young people that you are, with families of your own, is a great inspiration and blessing to me!

To my twelve grandchildren, I look at the beautiful bouquet of colors, gifts, talents, and abilities that you all possess and thank God for you every day, as my love for you all grows every day.

Introduction

This book of poems and prayers is dedicated to children all over the world.

The first poem, "I'm Happy Being Me," is written to inform children that we are all different and that's okay. I like being me, and I want you to like being you. It is important to me that we instill confidence in our children at an early age so that confidence will grow up in them internally as they grow naturally.

The last poem, "God Loves Me," will let children know that if God, who is all powerful, all knowing, and never makes a mistake loves them, then they are not a mistake. They are just the way they should be, and God loves them.

There is no need for jealously or envy if everyone knows that they are special in their own way. It's okay that we are all different, because if we were all the same, it would be boring and no fun at all.

The prayers are to let children know that there are simple words they can say to help them feel safe, protected, and loved.

The daily poems are to help children recognize that each day is special and should be looked at in that way, either in their reality or in their imagination.

My hope is that this book can truly help your child(ren) sincerely say, "I'm happy being me!"

I'm Happy Being Me

I am so happy being me
I am one of the happiest people
that you will ever see
Because I know that God slowly and
carefully shaped and formed me
God didn't make any mistakes
the day that He made me
I am wonderfully made
One of a kind, as you can clearly see
Say you are one of a kind, too
There is no one else around quite like you
What fun would this world be
If I looked just like you and
you looked just like me
God wanted us all to look different
Live in places that are different
Speak languages that are different
It's all a part of His great plan, you see
Now, I you can learn things from you
And you can learn things from me
Because we all have so much
to share and give
This world can be a great
place in which to live
Let's celebrate each other's differences
Let us join each other's hand
Let us lift them up with glee
Please be happy being you
Because I'm so happy being me

SUNDAY
TUESDAY
THU
MONDAY
FRIDAY

Every Day

Every morning of every day,
I will look to the Lord and I will say,
Thank You for this wonderful day!

I am your child, dear Lord.
In me please have Your way.
Take my hands,
Lead and guide me throughout this day,

In every way I want to please You.
I want to do what You say do
And say what You tell me to say.
Then I will bless someone else today
In a very special way.

Again, I say, thank You, Lord,
For such a wonderful day!

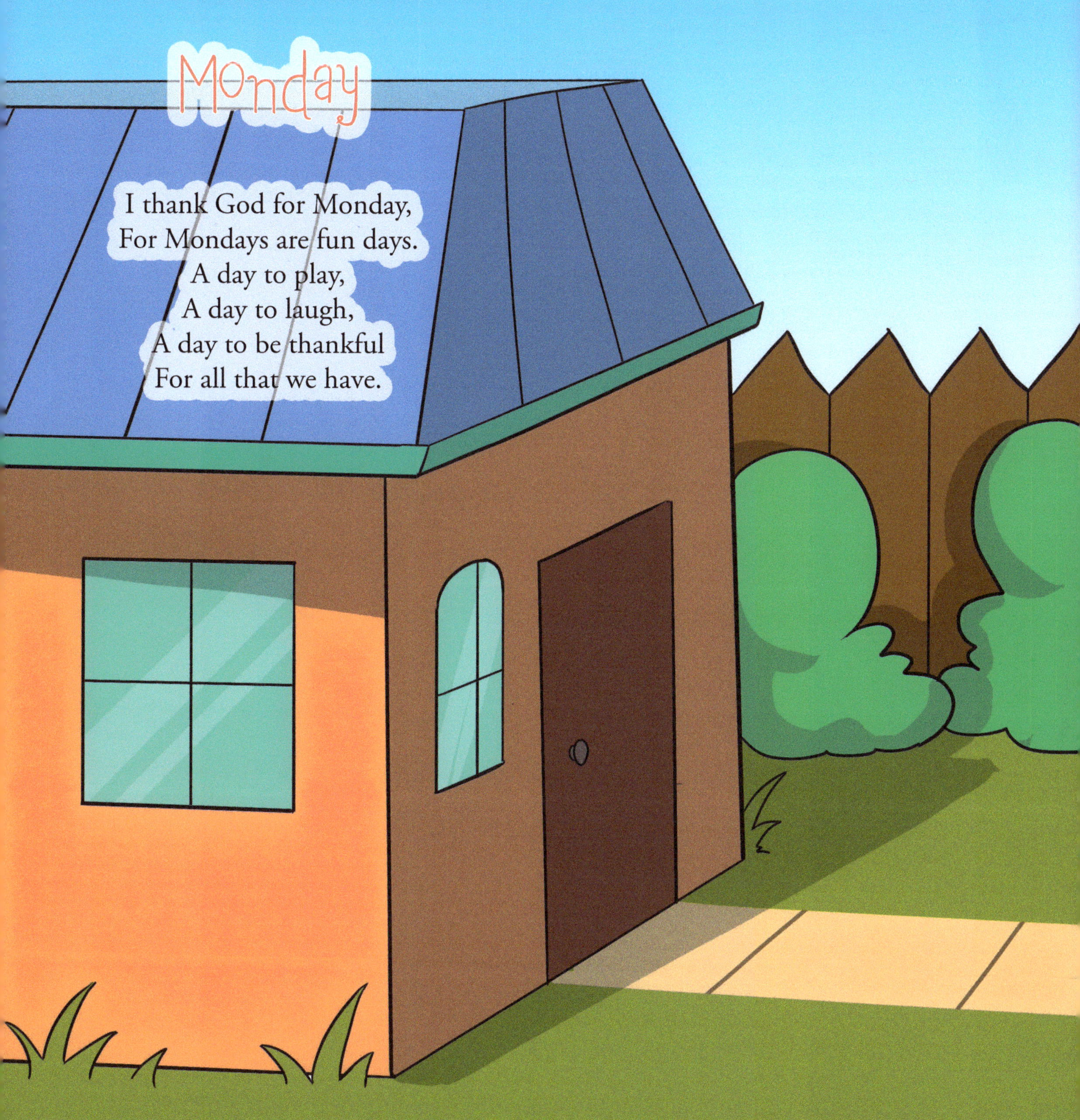

Monday

I thank God for Monday,
For Mondays are fun days.
A day to play,
A day to laugh,
A day to be thankful
For all that we have.

Tuesday

I thank God for Tuesday,
For Tuesday is a me and you day.
The two of us, or three,
maybe even the whole family,
Coming together as one.
Tuesday can be great fun!

Wednesday

I thank God for Wednesday,
For Wednesdays are Great Friends Day.
I have great friends at church,
I have great friends at home,
I have great friends in school, you see.
I am really thankful for the great friends
God has given me!

Thursday

I am excited about Thursday,
Because Thursday is my experiential day.
A day to try new things,
To learn new things.

A day to do old things in a whole new way,
A day to learn about new people,
The way they live and all their special ways.
A day to learn how they work
And even how they play.

I'll learn new words,
I'll learn new customs,
I'll learn new games to play,
I'll learn that tasks can be completed
Even when they are done in a completely different way.

Learning about different people,
Different countries,
Different cultures with different ways
Is a very cool way to spend my Thursday!

Friday

Oh, how I love Fridays!
The end-of-the-school-week day,
The beginning-of-the-weekend day,
The start of two days of play.
It all begins on Friday!

I'll stay up late tonight,
I'll sleep late tomorrow,
I'll go outside and play,
All my friends and me!

Friday is here!
Friday is here!
I'm as happy as I can be!

SCHOOL
15

Saturday

Saturday is a great day!
A fun day! A play day!
No school, no books, I'm free.
No schedules, no standing in line,
No hurry to get where I need to be,
No principals, no teachers,
No hall monitors watching over me.

I'm all on my own.
Now, let me see…
I'll play outside, I'll play inside.
I'll spend a lot of time with my pets.
I'll groom them and feed them—
Now, they're all set!

I'll jump, I'll run,
I'll ride my bike.
I'll even play some ball.
On this free day, I'll do it all.
But in the midst I'll hear my mother call.
I'll bathe, I'll eat,
And fast asleep in her arms I'll fall.
I love Saturdays!

Sunday

Dear Lord,
I thank You for Sunday.
Sunday is one of the best days.
A day to worship You.

A day to gather together
And say thank You!

Thank You
For all the great and wonderful
Things that you do.

A day to sing.
A day to pray.
A day to praise.
A day of fellowship too.

I Love My Beautiful Skin

I love the color of my beautiful skin,
I love being in the skin I'm in.
It was perfectly designed for me—
God does not make mistakes, you see!
He has a master plan,
A perfect plan,
For you and me!

In His plan He knows exactly
how He wants us to look
And what He wants us to be.

He shaped and formed us all,
He knew who we would be,
I think God just really loves variety!

He loves red and black,
Light brown, dark brown,
golden brown,
White and yellow, rosy pink, too!
One of these colors was
chosen just for me;
One was chosen just for you!

There is a purpose in this world,
A future, a destiny too!
A special place, just for me!
And a special place just for you!

As I Lay

As I lay me down to sleep,
I feel secure,
I feel at peace,
So my sleep is always sweet

The angels of the Lord
Are watching over me.
I'm safe in His arms,
And that's where I want to be!

Family Prayer

I thank You for my family,
I thank You for them all.
I thank You for the great big ones,
And I thank You for those that are small.
Please watch over them throughout the night
And guide them throughout the day.
They are so special to me.
And this is why for them I will pray.

23

God Loves Me

I know that God loves me!
I know because He made me different.
He made me different
From everyone else.
My hands and face are different;
My ears and nose are too.

My skin and hair are different;
That's why you don't look like me,
And I don't look like you.

I am specially made by God,
One of a kind, you see!
I don't have to look or
Be like anyone else.
I am so happy knowing that
God loves Me!